W9-BKD-892

A Look at

POP
aRT

Written by
Keli Sipperley

rourkeeducationalmedia.com

www.rourkeeducationalmedia.com

PHOTO CREDITS: Cover: © Christie's Images, © LUKE MACGREGOR; page 4-5, 7, 12, 21: © Associated Press; page 6-7, 9: © Burstein Collection; page 8: © Rune Hellestad; page 10-11: © LUKE MACGREGOR; page 13, 15: © Christie's Images; page 14: © Joe Potato Photo; page 16-17: © Albright-Knox Art Gallery; page 19: © Juli Hansen; page 20-21: © Dan Forer; page 22: © Ferran Traite Soler

Edited by Jill Sherman

Cover and Interior design by Tara Raymo

Library of Congress PCN Data

A Look at Pop Art / Keli Sipperley
(Art and Music)
ISBN 978-1-62169-875-3 (hard cover)
ISBN 978-1-62169-770-1 (soft cover)
ISBN 978-1-62169-975-0 (e-Book)
Library of Congress Control Number: 2013936784

Rourke Educational Media
Printed in the United States of America,
North Mankato, Minnesota

Also Available as:

Educational Media

rourkeeducationalmedia.com

customerservice@rourkeeducationalmedia.com • PO Box 643328 Vero Beach, Florida 32964

TABLE OF CONTENTS

art is everywhere

Is your lunch a work of art? It could be.

French Fries and Ketchup
by Claes Oldenburg, 1963

During the 1950s and 1960s, a new style of art emerged that changed the way people viewed fine art.

Artists in the United States and Great Britain turned the ordinary into the extraordinary by creating art based on American popular culture.

Swingeing London
by Richard Hamilton, 1972

Richard Hamilton
(1922–2011)

Works based on images like these
would have been considered "low art"
prior to the pop art movements.

Images of **celebrities** and advertisements were not considered worth displaying in a gallery or museum until the pop art movement began.

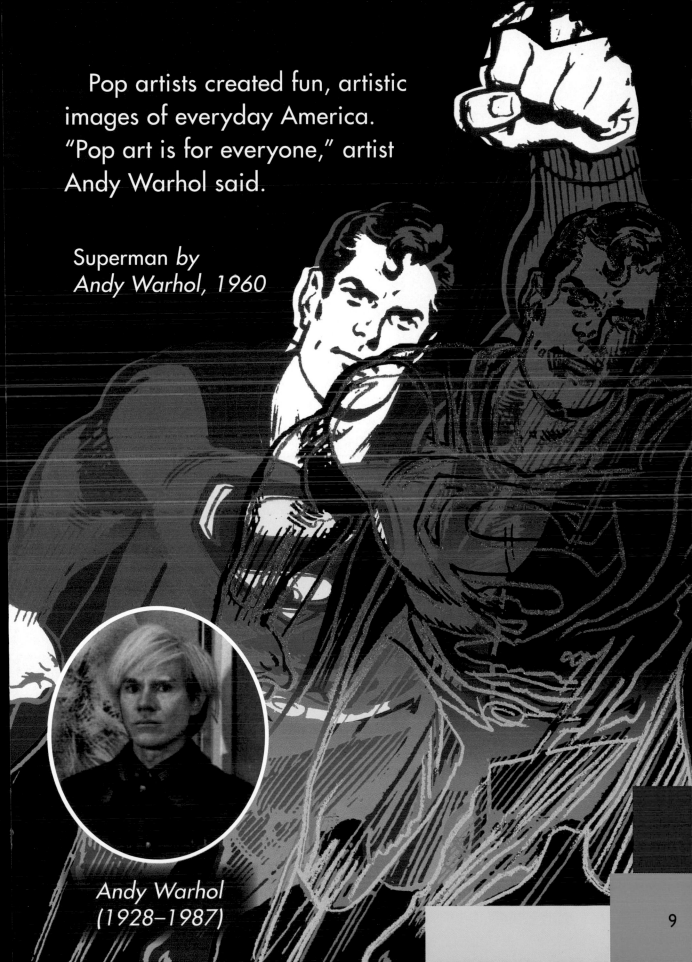

Pop artists created fun, artistic images of everyday America. "Pop art is for everyone," artist Andy Warhol said.

Superman by Andy Warhol, 1960

Andy Warhol (1928–1987)

SOUP STIRS THINGS UP

In 1962, Andy Warhol's 32 paintings of Campbell's Soup cans were displayed in a California art gallery.

The paintings rested on a shelf as if they were products on a grocery store shelf.

The soup can **exhibit** made Warhol famous and marked the **climax** of the pop art movement in America.

CHARACTERISTICS OF POP ART

Pop art paintings tend to have very bright colors, usually red, yellow, and blue. The images in pop art are flat like those in comic books.

Some artists also used **Ben-Day dots**, a method borrowed from comic book printing.

Roy Lichtenstein is famous for his paintings inspired by comic books.

Roy Lichtenstein
(1923–1997)

Sweet Dreams Baby!
by Roy Lichtenstein, 1962

Silk screens are also used in pop art. Andy Warhol used this commercial printing technique to reproduce an image multiple times.

Self portrait *by Andy Warhol, 1966*

Some pop artists used found materials, such as **discarded** television sets and telephones, to create their work. Others used photographs to make **collages**.

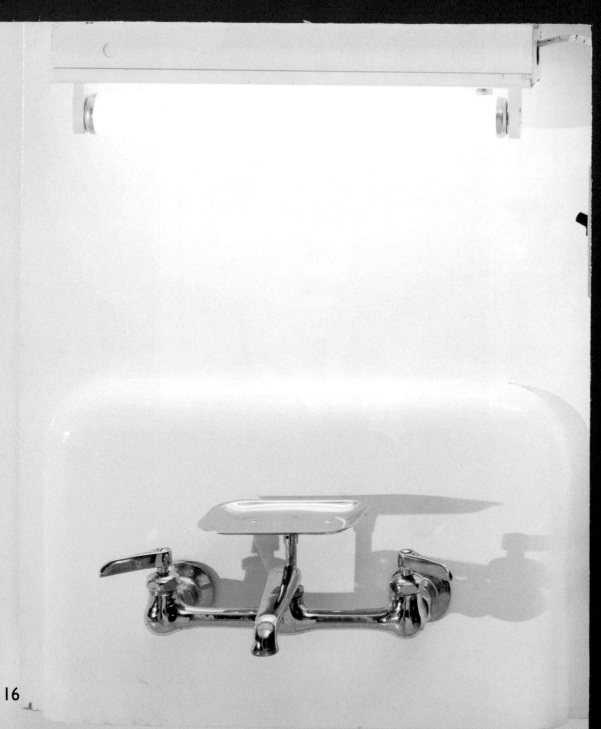

Still Life #20 by Tom Wesselmann, 1962

end of an era

In 1965, Andy Warhol said the pop art movement was over, but its impact remains strong today.

Modern artists still use the techniques made famous by Warhol and others to create everything from portraits to websites and greeting cards.

Pop art influences many artists today. Urban artists like Shepard Fairey use the silk screening techniques made popular by Warhol to create iconic images.

Hope *poster by Shepard Fairey, 2008*

POP ART LEAVES ITS MARK

Art by Romero Britto on display in a gallery.

Pop artists broke down the barriers between low art and fine art with their work based on things people see every day.

Romero Britto
(1963–)

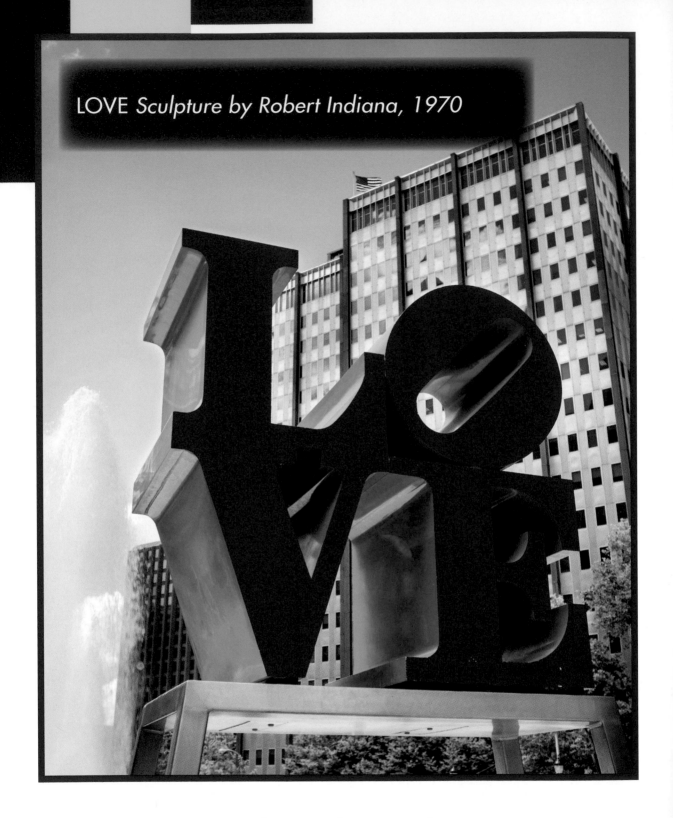

LOVE *Sculpture by Robert Indiana, 1970*

From soup cans to superheroes, the pop art movement showed the world that art is everywhere.

GLOSSARY

Ben-Day dots (ben-DAY dahts): dots used to add shading in comic books, newspapers, and other printed works

celebrities (suh-LEB-ri-teez): famous people, such as movie stars and singers

climax (KLYE-maks): the most important part

collages (kuh-LAHZHZ): pieces of art made by attaching different items such as photographs and objects to a surface

discarded (dis-KAHRD-ed): thrown away

exhibit (ig-ZIB-it): a public show of art or other interesting things

silk screens (silk skreenz): a method of printing that puts color through special fabric that only lets the paint go through certain areas

WEBSITES

www.moma.org/interactives/redstudio/popart

www.ducksters.com/history/art/pop_art.php

library.thinkquest.org/J001159/artstyle.htm

ABOUT THE AUTHOR

Keli Sipperley is a multimedia journalist and children's book author living in Tampa, Florida. She enjoys writing stories about interesting moments, fun places, and people who help others in their communities. She has two sons and two daughters who love reading and writing as much as she does.

Meet The Author!
www.meetREMauthors.com